All Scripture references taken from the KJV of the Holy Bible, unless otherwise indicated.

Why Do I Keep Meeting the *Same* Guy?

by Dr. Marlene Miles

Freshwater Press 2024

freshwaterpress9@gmail.com

ISBN: 978-1-963164-98-5

Paperback Version

Table of Contents

Why Do I Keep Meeting the Same <u>Same</u> *Guy*?

Freshwater Press, USA

The *Begats*

In the Bible there are lists of *begats* (KJV. We say, *begot*.) Genesis 4 begins the *begats* of the Bible, listing the generations from Adam to Noah—, and so on. Who procreated whom starts in Genesis and goes throughout the Bible to 1John. These lists are not to bore us, it is intentional, and it is very important. Who gave birth to whom, who got with whom, and how these generations progressed is among the purposes of the *begats*.

The Bible spends quite some time on the begats. Needing to know that kind of information is why there is Ancestry.com or 23 & Me and any other DNA searching services and platforms. People want to find out who their people are and where their people come from, especially people whose histories have been blurred, missing, or even erased. Most of us want to know how our chain of *begetting* came about.

In the New Testament, in the Book of Matthew we see the begats forward to the generations that led up to the birth of Jesus Christ. Looking in the other direction, we can also see Jesus' connections all the way back to Adam and Eve.

The begats might be both the most boring and confusing part of the Bible, but it is necessary. The begats throughout the Bible is the family tree, it is the story of the **FOUNDATION** of Jesus Christ. The Bible is the Volume of the Book where it is written of Jesus, And the *begats* describe how Jesus' foundation came to be as it is by telling us who the people are who were in it. Of course, for spiritual reasons, we must know His lineage, but when we look deeper into the people who progenerated Jesus of Nazareth, we can see much by knowing something of His predecessors who formed His foundation.

And what has this to do with you?

Everything.

What does this have to do with the title of this book?

Everything.

Once I asked a fellow about his grandparents. He said he didn't know who they were and asked me, what difference does it make?

It makes all the difference.

What do the *begats* in your family look like? What does your family tree look like? Not just who is in it, but what kind of people were they? What did they do? What God did they serve? How did they live? It matters, it really matters.

Ladies, your foundation has everything to do with the kinds of guys you are meeting. Men, the same applies to you – the kinds of women you meet, the kinds of women you are attracted to have to do with the *begats* of both of your family lines, on both sides, and each parent's spiritual foundation. **Attraction is physical, but it is also spiritual.**

It could very well be that because of the *begats* of your foundation you will meet people who fit into certain criteria for you to procreate with.

Try as you may, without Jesus Christ, you will only attract the *kinds* of guys that are in your foundation, and the types that your foundation fosters and calls forth. You keep meeting the same kinds of guys because of your foundation.

Additionally, you may be meeting the same kinds of guys because there is a whole plot against you getting married.

Why? Why does the devil not want you married?

Because **God said BE FRUITFUL AND MULTIPLY.** If you can't fulfill the first thing God said to do, then it will be a struggle or an impossibility to receive what else is in that verse, as well as what else is in the entire Bible.

And God blessed them, and God said unto them, Be fruitful, and multiply, and replenish the earth, and subdue it: and have dominion over the fish of the sea, and over the fowl of the air, and over every living thing that moveth upon the earth. (Genesis 1:28)

There is a demonic plot against you getting married, being fruitful, multiplying, having children—having righteous seed. Not only that, but there is also an entire satanic plot against you having the rest of the stuff in that verse.

It would be the devil who would send you wrong guys that you are not interested in or attracted to as potential mates and spouses. Yes, so you won't want to marry them. It could be in the plan of the devil to send those with certain negative traits that will irritate and frustrate you, and ultimately derail your life and destiny.

It could be the *spirit* in you attracts a certain *spirit* in that other person and the devil would be happy if the two of you joined forces to make those two *spirits* join and be exponentially stronger, but to the negative. This could be why you are meeting the same type of guy over and again—a demonic set up.

The only way to fight this is to be in Christ --, **_all in_**. And your spouse, too.

But I'm Blessed

God has blessed you. What does that even mean?

When we bless one another, we may help each other, we may give someone a gift or something they have need of. We can bless people verbally, with words and or with tangible things. Someone could hand you a gift and along with those words of blessing. Or, someone could bless you with words only, invoking or imploring **God** to provide the intangible thing, such as peace or whatever they are wishing or declaring over your life.

The Lord bless thee, and keep thee:

The Lord make his face shine upon thee, and be gracious unto thee:

The Lord lift up his countenance upon
thee, and give thee peace.
(Numbers 6:24-26).

Or, they could be invoking **God** to
give you tangible goods that you may
need, or want, to show that you are
blessed.

We bless food before we eat it, which
means that we are sanctifying and giving
thanks for it. Blessing someone could set
them aside for special use, as parents in
the Bible blessed their firstborn sons who
opened the womb.

BTW: *Bless your heart* is not a
blessing; it is a snarky insult.

We are blessed to be a blessing. God
says, ***In blessing, I will bless thee.***

In the Garden with Adam and Eve,
GOD is doing the blessing, so God is not
just wishing something over those He is
blessing. He is actually blessing, in the
now, in real time. God also blesses

prophetically. Blessings of God sometimes have requirements. We could be blessed, prophetically, and God gives us time to meet the criteria that He has set forth to receive those blessings.

God knows, and He outlines it in the Bible. We have to look for it, search it out, and be obedient to do it.

The blessings of God maketh rich and He adds no sorrow with it. This is one way to know that the blessing is from God--, no sorrow with it. There are fake blessings, there are make-believe "blessings", and then there are just wishes. The Word also says that we are **blessed to be a blessing**.

If we are not blessed, can we *be* a blessing? Can we bless another?

When you bless someone and really mean it, you actually bless them, saying, *I bless you in the Name of the Lord.*

If you are blessed of God to be a blessing, then you are blessed of God. When we bless for real, in real time, we hand someone the thing that blesses them. Or we can, in authority issue forth intangible blessings of the Lord upon that other person as long as we are in Christ and have authority to do so.

> Neither do they which go by say, The blessing of the LORD *be* upon you: we bless you in the name of the LORD.
> (Psalm 129:8)

God blessed them and said be fruitful and multiply. God blessed them: That is past tense which means He did it, said it, spoke it, gave it, imparted it, already. So, you're blessed, but if you are not being fruitful and multiplying then how will you have the rest of what is in that verse?

- Being able to subdue the Earth
  - o Bible folks were farmers so subduing the Earth meant you'd have a good crop and prosperous career. You'd

have enough for your family.

- Having dominion over everything: fish of the sea, birds of the air, and all living things that move on the Earth.
  - o Consider this to mean a spiritual dominion, unless we are going to go all Dr. Doolittle. Dominion over animals doesn't literally mean to talk to birds and fish and tell them what to do, although it can mean that.

Seriously, it means we are to take and have and walk in spiritual dominion. Spiritually we take dominion over *spiritual* things in the sea and in the air and on the Earth.

I would suppose that being fruitful and multiplying in the context of marriage means taking dominion together as a married couple. This dominion means two together which is why the devil doesn't want folks successfully married because two together can kick some spiritual situations out into outer darkness.

There's power in one; one can put a thousand angels to flight, but two can put 10,000 to flight. **That's why the devil doesn't want you in covenant marriage with your Kingdom spouse, and connected together.**

One can put a thousand to flight and two, 10,000. Therefore, if one is a BB gun, then two together is a bazooka. This is a no brainer. If you were in a real war in the natural, would you want two allies to join together and fight against you, or is one at a time enough? That's why the devil would not want two together either --, especially two together with a bazooka that they know how to use. Furthermore, when two become one, God commands **many more blessings and even more favor** when that man finds his wife.

Devil warfare against you is not about your happiness and your fulfillment. It is not about you finding a husband or a wife; it's about **POWER**. It's about your purpose and destiny.

This is why you keep meeting the same folks over and over, instead of the right one or the kind that you believe, or know you are supposed to be with. This could be why they call getting married after some certain time has passed, *settling down*. The operative word here is *settling*. **Settling with the wrong one, or no one, with no POWER is what this anti-marriage warfare is about.**

This could be why the devil keeps presenting those good looking but *not-for-you,* or *not- for-long term* kinds of dates as marriage opportunities because he KNOWS that you with that person will amount to **NO power** against him and no threat to him. The devil is ever hoping that the people of God will *settle* for what the devil is sending to them. You've heard folks say, *You surely won't find anyone better; there's not a lot out here.*

That doesn't sound like an active choice to me, that sounds like a consolation prize.

Be sure to look deeply spiritually before you decide if a potential spouse is attractive to you or not. **Be different**: Be attracted to a person spiritually first, then check out their physical and other credentials.

God Is Not a Dating Service

God is not interested in you meeting guys or girls **to date**. He is interested in you getting with the one you're supposed to be married to and you two becoming one and firing that bazooka at the works of the devil.

God is not a dating service. God doesn't make sure you have people to date. So, if you are praying to God for a date or a casual mate, you are praying in the wrong direction.

God does make divine connections, and divine appointments and you should aspire to meet those divine appointments, and not miss any visitations of the Lord. But God is not setting you up with 5 or 8 different people to date so you can pick one. The one that is the cutest, the one you like the most, or the one that you think has the most money, the best car, or the most to offer you.

No.

In the Bible God sent one to get one and they married that one, but it was the right one. God does not waste time.

Dating and playing around, entertaining your flesh is wasting time, and it is sin.

So, if and when you are serious about marriage, and you've done your spiritual work to be ready you can meet the right one. Else, why would God be in that? Why would God be in you meeting people to date that you won't marry because you don't even want to get married? But you just want to date somebody really good for your convenience, for your emotions so you won't be lonely, and for your flesh?

Why would God even want you to meet anyone at all, if you don't want to get married? Even if you are pretending to look for a spouse while playing the field, you may trick some folks, for a season, but you won't trick God.

God is not interested in you meeting people to *sin* with. This could be why you keep meeting these **same** people that you are not really interested in, over and over. It could be why you keep meeting all these people with serious flaws, or baggage and they are terribly unattractive as their whole package goes. God's not in this, that's why it looks like you're getting the rejects.

Oh pls.

If you've rejected the plan of God yourself, that is to get married, be fruitful and multiply, then you will meet others who have also rejected God and His plan for two people.

You are not serious about marriage, but you just want a "friend" with benefits? The devil has that service, not God. You are praying to the wrong *person*.

When you are sinning, especially sexual sin, you are indeed **LAYING** a foundation. You are indeed laying something in your foundation or toward your foundation. Your foundation is directing your life, and that includes your dating and marital life. Ask God, believe God, have faith and wait to meet the right person, but are you dealing with, or have you dealt with your foundation?

The devil, however, will distract you with dates and frogs and foolishness until you're 100 years old if you don't do something about it, if your intentions are impure--, until you do something about yourself and get serious. If you are not dealing with your foundation, you will get the same results over and again, except by some miracle of

God. Our Father can do the miraculous, but we live by faith, not just by signs, and wonders, and miracles. Signs and wonders are for sinners and unbelievers; the just shall live by Faith. Amen.

Every time you sin, especially sexual sin, you are *laying* alright—you are laying another stone, a rock of offense into your foundation; your foundation is getting laid, too. Laid with iniquity.

When you sin, you are sinning for yourself and for your children and your grandchildren--, every time you sin. Unless you repent, really and fully repent, the iniquity of it is going into the family foundation. It's almost understandable how youthful lust can cause a person to fall into sin, especially before you have children. But after an innocent child is looking you in the face, how any of us can go out and sin against God, and against our spouse and that beautiful little child is a lot harder to understand. When you make that deposit, you are depositing iniquity right into your family's foundation. Especially sexual sin, you are also sinning against your own body.

Get Serious

Until you get saved, and get all in Christ and begin to purge and heal your foundation, the one that you've been dealt by your ancestors and parents is the one you've got. That FOUNDATION is running the show; it is running your life.

That foundation has all the iniquity that your parents and ancestors stored up in it. Even when they thought no one was looking or no one would know, iniquity is like the *Internet*—it doesn't forget.

The devil doesn't want you getting married to bring forth righteous seed. If you think about it, 100 or so years on the Earth is but a vapor in the timeline of God, so you have to leave somebody or some people here to carry the baton that you are currently carrying. You are doing spiritual work in the Earth, right?

Okay, so you leave a righteous seed. That's what God makes, that's what He creates, expects, looks for and uses for Kingdom work.

How to bring forth righteous seed: saved husband, saved wife, CORRECT CONNECTION AND ENVIRONMENT FOR CONCEPTION, THAT IS GOD IS IN IT and no other *little g gods*. There are no conception *rituals*, just you and your spouse and God. A saved husband and a saved wife, both with righteous, solid spiritual foundations will conceive and bring forth righteous children. That is what you should be bringing forth in your being fruitful and multiplying.

This righteous seed--, doesn't just wander around the Earth doing whatever it wants with no teaching or guidance. You will minister to your seed daily, pray for him/her daily, train them up in the way they should go, and raise them up in the fear and the admonition of the Lord.

All else is children of flesh. Sorry.

Your Foundation Is Speaking

Your foundation is dictating your life, it is running your life, outside of Christ. If Christ is not in you and you are not in Christ, then your foundation is running the whole thing. Whatever your ancestors or parents have put in your foundation, that is what is being dictated to you. Your foundation is speaking from the first moment that you are born and all of your life.

If you find out that you have a faulty foundation, then you will have a faulty life. If you have to start all over again to build a proper and Godly foundation, then do it. Make Jesus the cornerstone of your foundation.

You could be the absolute best at whatever you have in your heart to do but with a faulty foundation, you may find that you do not rise above your family members who do absolutely nothing in life. Are the family members pulling you down? Is there household witchcraft? No? Then, they are not. Are you all in collective captivity? Possibly. Are you all working from the same foundation? Yup. That is the common denominator.

You have 5 diplomas, degrees, or certificates in your field, have been working three jobs for 20 years but you have the same results in the end as the sibling who has done little to nothing all their life. Why?

Foundation.

If you plant seeds in a field with faulty soil, you will get no plants and harvest, or little plants and little harvest. You and your sibling have the same field, absent Christ, so whatever you do yields the same or very similar results.

Behold, I lay in Zion for a *foundation* a stone ~ a precious cornerstone.
(Isaiah 28:16)

We like to think that Scripture is about the cornerstone for the Church, and it is. But it is also the cornerstone for your own foundation, your personal individual and family bloodline foundation also.

Other *foundation* can no man lay than that which is laid, which is Jesus Christ.
(1 Corinthians 3:10)

So, why do you keep meeting the same type of guys over and over again? You may have said or heard others ask, *Is there nothing out here? How do you meet a nice person anymore?* Depends on what your intentions are. Depends on whether you're fully in Christ or not. Depends on your spiritual foundation; what are you working with? If you are, then God can pick out your spouse. If you're not saved, or not fully in Christ, and not really planning to get married, then your foundation is picking out your *dates.*

When GOD chooses your mate, that's another whole thing. When GOD blesses you and sees that you are walking in the blessing He will step in and answer your prayers. A person could be blessed and still *reject* the blessing by rejecting God. But when God blesses you and you are walking upright before Him, He will pick out someone blessed for you for Godly Purpose. It is not simply for your entertainment or your prideful bragging rights.

You do end up enjoying each other and having a good life, but that is not the main purpose. The main purpose is for **Purpose**, and it is for destiny.

It doesn't mean that it won't be the best absolute most gorgeous most everything you like about a person, but you have got to be serious about God and about marriage and family and righteous seed, and about the purpose and destiny that God has put in you.

If not, God is not getting in that.

Did people have trouble finding a wife in the olden days? Solomon didn't, but if he had 1000 wives, what did 999 guys who may have been looking for their wife *do*? Solomon could have had those guys' wives over at the palace while those guys could find no one to marry. Solomon took that honest; didn't the Prophet Nathan tell David that he took one man's only *ewe lamb*? (2 Samuel 2:3) Solomon could have taken the only ewe of 999 fellows in or around his kingdom.

Ruth was looking for a kinsman redeemer and she had to, in my opinion, do some stunts to win him. Perhaps it was easier back in those days, maybe a guy just had to knock a girl over the head with a club and then she was his woman. Perhaps a woman just had to seduce a guy and then he was married to her. It doesn't work either of those ways, these days, and you shouldn't want it to. Spiritually, goes into does equal married, but how many guys can you say that to and they'll say, Oh wow, *I guess we are married now*?

Uh, *like none.*

The 7000 Club

Yet you may keep asking, where are all the *good guys*? How come others have found good spouses and not me?

Yet God will say, I've got 7000 that haven't bowed a knee. **God will not let you play with HIS and certainly not HIS BEST.** Which may explain why you keep meeting the *same ole, same ole* and not God's blessed and God's best.

Yet I have left me seven thousand in Israel, all the knees which have not bowed unto Baal, and every mouth which hath not kissed him.
(1 Kings 19:18)

But what saith the answer of God unto him? I have reserved to myself seven thousand men, who have not bowed the

knee to the image of Baal.
(Romans 11:4)

Where are those 7000?

And, I'm asking you: Are you among the 7000? Are you among God's best? I pray you are. And if you are, God will get into your finding and or being *found* by your Kingdom spouse.

God is saving the good ones for the ones who are serious – not desperate, but serious.

Yet we all have sinned and fallen short of the Glory of God, so if we fell into sin, have we gotten back up and repented? Then AMEN and we are still in the race.

God has 7000 set aside. Could it be that perhaps because of your foundation, you are not supposed to meet any of those 7000? We'd all do better to be sure we've met the one, JESUS Christ before trying to meet someone to marry.

No, I'm not condemning you or saying anything is wrong with you, I am repeating that attraction is spiritual, not just physical. Of course, as flesh beings, we think it's physical, but it is so much deeper than that. This is why you hear some women say, *You picked her? Her? She's not even better looking than I am!*

Told you--- attraction is spiritual.

So why aren't you meeting or supposed to meet any of the set-aside guys?

Well, it depends on your criteria, what is a desirable fellow? What is a desirable lady? The spiritually correct guys may not even have the looks that appeal to you, but you can only see flesh. When you cannot see the goodness and the value in a person, then you are showing your carnality. If you are picking dates or potential mates by how they look only ---, God is not in that.

Or, maybe God is in it and the divine connection He had for you didn't match your physical specs so you passed them right by, or maybe even met them and passed them over.

Why do you keep meeting the same *guy*? Is it because you haven't changed your criteria since high school? Are you covered or veiled? Do the good guys not even see you? Do you even know a good one when you see them, or meet them? Covering cast or evil veil could be a curse in a bloodline. Haven't you seen a family of gorgeous people yet none of them or few are married? People may see them, but they don't see them as beautiful, or handsome, or as marriage material. *Spirit spouse* is known for covering its victim.

Your foundation. Your foundation may need work, it may need a lot of work.

1. Father, remove any covering cast from me that I may see and be seen by divine connections you have for me, in the Name of Jesus.

2. Lord, remove and burn the evil veil over my glory, in the Name of Jesus.

Pre-empted, Pre-*emptied*?

Some like to argue that we are not predestined. But we are predestined by God for good things. Fearfully and wonderfully made, crowned with Glory and Honor. Remember, God said about us that, *It is good* and then He blessed us.

> For we are his workmanship, created in
> Christ Jesus unto good works, which
> God hath before ordained that we
> should walk in them.
> (Ephesians 2:10)

We are predestined to good works and to walk in a certain successful path that leads to destiny. But that predestination can be pre-empted by evil and by pollution in our foundation. Evil spirits that are in our souls could have come from our foundation, that is what is meant by "our father's house" that is, things we inherit. Spirits that should not be in a foundation are any that are not the Holy Spirit of God, to include *spirit spouse* which we have mentioned and will discuss further later on in this book.

It could be **pre-empted** by evil handwriting against any of us, and that handwriting is in our foundations.

Blotting out the handwriting of ordinances that was against us, which was contrary to us, and took it out of the way, nailing it to his cross;
(Colossians 2:14)

In your foundation are blessings (hopefully) That's the predestined foundation that God has for us. If Jesus is the Chief Cornerstone, then God has laid the foundation. That's the full intention.

(More on this later).

40

Human Interference

Any curses, any diabolical prayers, any soul-tied revenge voices speaking against your future relationships is human interference. Astral projecting humans assaulting you in the night as a *spirit spouse* is human interference.

Break every soul tie. Forgive and make peace with every ex. Banish every stalker of every kind, especially spiritual stalkers--, get them out of your life. (Read **Astral Projected Spirit Spouse, DIE!** And pray the prayers at the end of that book.)

Be at peace with anyone who has any authority to speak over your life or into your life. You might be surprised at who that is. Your parents? Yes. Your elder relatives such as aunts and uncles? Yup -- - the *village*. It not only takes a village to raise a child, as they say, but people in that village can raise hell in your life. You'd better be in Christ, stay in Christ and stay prayed up.

Your siblings? Yup—, anyone related to you or lives with you and has access to you and the details of your life. Your best friend and confidante. Your roommate in college.

Those who don't live with you such as your teacher(s). Your pastor or anyone who has any type of spiritual authority over you. Your haters. Jealous fake friends.

If anyone has issued an active curse against you, or even a curse from back in the day by saying something in what you thought was jest, but it seems to have followed you into adulthood, break that curse, in the Name of Jesus.

3. I break every word curse ever spoken over me, and any part of my life, especially anything concerning my relationships, marriage, education, health, success, and children, in the Name of Jesus.

4. I renounce every word curse I've ever spoken over myself in ignorance, defiance, or in rebellion, in any part of my life, especially anything concerning my relationships, marriage, education, health, success, and children, in the Name of Jesus.

5. Every scattering word spoken over my relationships and my ability to draw proper suitors to my life, be canceled by the power in the Blood of Jesus.

6. Every evil and diabolical, soulish word curse spoken by any unforgiving or bitter, jealous ex, be canceled right now by Fire, by Fire, by Fire, in the Name of Jesus.

7. Every word curse spoken over my success in relationships by any *blind witch*, let those words expire now, in the Name of Jesus.

8. If any witch, warlock, wizard or any worker of evil has put my relationships, marriage, family, or children contemporaneously or prophetically on any evil altar, be removed from every evil altar and be set free, in the Name of Jesus.

9. My life, take the sacrifice of Christ and be renewed, redeemed and restored to original estate and the original plan that God had for my life when He formed me and said, *It is Good*, in the Name of Jesus.

10. Every ancestral curse, generational curse, family curse and individual curse, fall to the ground as dead works as the power of any evil covenant that allows your presence in my life or foundation is broken by the power in the Blood of Jesus.

Amen.

It Is Written

God speaks, and what God speaks it is **Written**. It is written, it is written – GOD speaks all the blessings and the plans for our lives. It is written in our foundation. and what He speaks is written—the Ten Commandments, for example is definitely written in the Spirit. God was gracious enough to write it down for Moses to give to the people, but the first rendering was destroyed. God had to repeat Himself.

A hallmark of a teacher is that he or she repeats himself. In the New Testament Jesus was called Rabboni which interpreted means, *teacher*. While it is disrespectful to be so hardheaded that our teachers must repeat themselves, graciously, they do. Well, unless they tell you to go look it up--, which is the same as saying, *It is written.* They got that from Jesus.

Teachers are usually very patient to teach; God even repeated what He had already said and written to be sure we get those Ten Commandments.

Jeremiah was speaking a Thus saith the Lord and his Scribe, Baruch was recording what he said. King Jehoiakim didn't like what God had said so he burned the scroll. Jeremiah sat with Baruch again and re-dictated what God had said all over again. (Jeremiah 36).

What GOD says stands: **IT IS WRITTEN**. If you don't like it, too bad. God is Sovereign; what He says goes.

Scribes were very influential back in Bible days, as historians they recorded things. They wrote them down.

Jesus, when He was tempted in the Wilderness, He said, **It is written.**

The enemy copies what God says and does and puts Post-Its and other written nasty ordinances against man in writing as well, and he puts that stuff in our foundations if we are not careful. If we are sinning, if we are not *watching* they can get into our foundations. These evil ordinances haunt a bloodline for generations by virtue of being in the foundation. That's the kind of corruption and pollution that is in what should be a Godly foundation with Jesus as the cornerstone.

The cornerstone sets the dimensions and the materials to be used in a foundation. The cornerstone sets the build, the plumbline.

Our foundations should be beautiful, righteous, Godly. But, if we are not careful, if we are not watching, if we are not prayerful, if we are sinning. If we are not wise and discerning, sometimes, we, or our ancestors) let things into our foundation. If the one that dealt it doesn't get it out, most often humans think that it's forgotten—rather out of sight, out of mind. Maybe, but it is not out of the foundation just because a human disguised it, hid it, or forgot about it.

Why?

Because it is written.

The devil wrote it down too.

Why?

So, he wouldn't forget it; so he could enforce it. So he could bring trauma and drama into your life at the most inopportune time and exact the most damage to you, your life, your destiny, your future.

Folks, if we are not vigilant to find out what is in our foundation, the devil may try to sneak any number of things into the foundation. If we are not paying attention, he may be able to put anything he wants in there. If we are not wise, we may agree to let evil things into our own life and into our own foundations. Hidden initiations… Man, we didn't even know that we did anything wrong or got initiated into anything. Well, when we walk by sight only, we think that only the traps that we **see** are the real snares. Nope. There are hidden nets and entrapments.

There it is in your foundation, your children and your *children's* children; your bloodline may get caught in this. You are the child of somebody, and you are the grandchild of somebody, so whatever slipped in there may be something that you are walking out right now.

Don't you have to fan flies away from good food on a summer picnic? Ants? Same thing. God prewrote our foundation when He made man, blessed man and said, ***It is good***. So here come the spiritual gnats and *what not* trying to gnaw away at the foundation that God has created for us.

If we are paying no attention, if we are out in the world doing whatever we want and paying no attention to spiritual things, the devil can just about put anything he wants into a foundation. Now it's in your bloodline, in your family waiting for your children and your *children's* children. And, you are the child of somebody. You are the grandchild of somebody; so whatever may have slipped into the family foundation with your ancestors, you may be walking it out right now. This could explain why you are not meeting the type that you think you should be meeting, but you are meeting some *different* guys, if anyone at all. the enemy copies what God does, and he writes too, only he puts in Evil Ordinances in our foundations.

11.   Lord, in the Name of Jesus BLOT out with the Blood of Jesus every evil ordinance recorded against me and my generations in my foundation.

12.   Holy Ghost Fire, cleanse and heal my foundation, in the Name of Jesus.

What is written in your foundation? Look in the natural world and take note of what you are going through. Spiritually map it, figure it out-- If you see the same thing happening to more than one person in your family, that's a pattern. Then you can guess what has been happening in the generations leading up to you. now you see why your **begats** are so important.

Yeah, we get tired, but the Laws of God are supposed to be written on the tablets of our heart, that I might not sin against You. (Proverbs 7:3)

Human DNA can hold 3 GIGABYTES of data. That's more than your computer can hold probably. 3 Gigabytes of data is written into your foundation. So, it gets into each human's DNA, what gets into the next generation and the next? It is written, it is recorded so it's not forgotten. It's going in there.

Well, what gets weeded out?

Everything gets in the next generation unless you do something about it spiritually. Unless you blot it out with the Blood of Jesus. Unless you cleanse it with Holy Ghost Fire… Unless you speak and decree against it, it will continue to be in your foundation. Until you do something spiritually, in prayer and spiritual warfare. Then what was always in your people will remain in your people.

What was always in your bloodline will remain in your bloodline.

Who are your people? Who are, (or were) your grandparents? Who *begat* you? Who were your ancestors and what did they do?

- Were they saved?
- How did they interact with people?
- Did they walk upright before God?
- Were they evil? Were they blessed?
- Did they make devil deals? In greed or desperation?

- ## DID THEY DIE OWING SPIRITUAL DEBT TO THE DEVIL?

It's possible that you don't know the answer to those questions. It is possible that any of us may be left shrugging our shoulders. But we don't have to guess if it is written. It is written down somewhere and perhaps it is written down everywhere, spiritually speaking. God keeps careful records, and the devil is just looking for something to trap a man on, so he has recorded any spiritual debt against your parents as well.

Why?

To accuse the brethren, to ensnare you. To take from you and punish you and your bloodline; he comes not but to steal, kill and destroy. And GUESS WHO WILL PAY if your ancestors left spiritual debt? The next generation or the one after that; and that could be you. You are your parents' next generation.

54

So, we pray and ask the Holy Spirit to reveal to us the stuff that is in our foundation that needs to be cast out, burnt out, weeded out, flushed out, uprooted, and prayed out.

Why?

Because the next generation up to pay for spiritual debt in your family **bloodline** could be you. Or you can wait for negative events and negative manifestations, such as why you're not meeting who you believe or know that you are supposed to meet for a spouse. If there are anti-progress, anti-prosperity, anti-marriage or marriage failure curses, clauses, or covenants in your foundation--, that could be why you are suffering in any area of your life today. It could be why you don't have the career you know you're supposed to have. It could be why your health is different than you know it should be. Jesus died for us that we would be saved, not be in poverty or be sick, but to be in health and prosper. Do you have all that?

God blessed them and said, *Be fruitful and multiply.* To have the blessing and keep it is integral to being fruitful and multiplying. Also, being fruitful and multiplying is integral in the blessing and staying blessed because you are in obedience. What parent doesn't like obedience? Blessed. Married. Fruitful and multiplying–, a cognitive test? No; commandments from God. He is our parent and our obedience pleases Him. As well, He takes pleasure in our prosperity. So, this is a win-win.

13.   My life, take the sacrifice of Christ and be renewed, redeemed, and restored to original estate and the original plan that God had for my life when He formed me and said, *It is Good,* in the Name of Jesus.

14.   Lord, I take the sacrifice of Christ and the Blood of Jesus to blot out every evil handwriting upon my foundation and upon my life and generations, in the Name of Jesus.

15.   On my newly restored foundation Lord, rewrite as You had to do the Ten Commandments for Moses and re-speak as You did for Baruch in the Book of Jeremiah the unpolluted, uncorrupted plan for my life, in the Name of Jesus.

16.   Rewrite my story Lord, in the Name of Jesus.

17.   Rewrite every word on the 3-gigabyte foundation of my life to my good and to the Praise of Your Glory, in the Name of Jesus.

Spiritual Debt

Jesus came to Earth so that we would have an abundant life. Do we have that? And if not, why?

Did someone in your bloodline die owing spiritual debt? That is iniquity. Debt is when you still owe for something you already received. Spiritual debt is when you received something tangible in the natural, or spiritually in the spirit, but you haven't paid spiritually for it. When your ancestors derived a benefit from the devil or any of his franchisee idol *gods*, but they haven't paid for it, the BLOODLINE owes. The evil ordinance of a warrant in debt is posted on the foundation of that family.

However, it is invisible until some bad stuff starts happening in the natural. Then you suffer, or you figure it out and get it out of your foundation.

The devil sells spiritual stuff for spiritual pay. He sells physical stuff for physical stunts and rituals AND spiritual pay. Anything anyone gets from the devil there is something spiritual to pay, often in the form of blood. The sacrifices he wants are blood sacrifices.

Taking things from you such as money, houses, relationships is PUNISHMENT; what he wants is blood and if you have not given him blood, he exacts punishments in the natural world that you can feel as pain, losses, and disappointments. Taking money does not settle the debt. **The currency is <u>not</u> money, even if you or your ancestor got money from the devil.**

So, based on what you're going through and what is happening in your life—provided you <u>know</u> you didn't do anything to cause your current situations, marital, disappointing financial, etc. And you know that no witch or occultist sent this to you, then you must deduce that it's ancestral. It's generational, it is foundational; *it is written* in your foundation.

How much do you owe? How much does your bloodline owe? Possibly everything. Anything you get from the devil usually costs everything and that means into time as well. So, devil deals are made with men with now in mind. Devil deals are made with the devil with the devil thinking of eternity in mind.

Mankind, what are we doing?

18.   Lord in the Name of Jesus, by the Blood of Jesus blot out every evil ordinance in my foundation.

19.   Remove all iniquity from my bloodline in the Name of Jesus.

You don't really know, what your ancestors did. We can only know by what you are going through in your life, and we deduce what must be in there based on our current suffering. Unless you know you caused all of this yourself. In which case you repent. Repent regularly and often. Repent every day, anyway. Repent for your parents and ancestors as well.

Who your ancestors were is important because they contributed to your DNA. Your DNA contains 3 gigabytes of information in it--, that's a lot of writing.

That information includes what your life should look like. Successes. Limitations. Repayment schedule of spiritual debt. Let's not kid ourselves, demonic spiritual debt is never repaid. The loan is *serviced* with interest and penalties, duties and responsibilities of owing the debt.

We know that DNA coding includes info such as your eye color, your hair color, how tall you are and all about your physical structure. But that's not all that's in there. Your DNA determines how all that stuff is expressed. As well, what is in your blood and your foundation, includes your blessings, your cursings, and, any evil plantations, any evil ordinances. You inherit not just your beautiful eyes and tall stature, and good looks and smarts, but you could inherit spiritual iniquity if your ancestors died owing spiritual debt. Where you should go, where you can't go is spiritually encoded in your foundation. How much you can prosper in life and how little. It's all in there; you've got to get the evil stuff out.

20. Lord, cancel every debt, by the Blood of Jesus, in the Name of Jesus.

21. Let me owe no man anything, except to love them, in the Name of Jesus.

22.   Lord let all iniquity and spiritual debt be expunged, with prejudice, from my foundation, that the enemies I see today shall not come up against me again, in the Name of Jesus. Amen.

God Is Visiting

God is visiting to the 3rd and the 4th generations of those that LOVE HIM. If your family is not saved, more generations than that, possibly are considered. The spiritual stuff that's in there is what God is looking at when He visits.

If no one has bothered to pray and fast and do warfare to get that mess out of a foundation, then God, who hates that devilish stuff, will have to judge it.

So, it is incumbent upon you to find out what's in your foundation whether what is in your foundation is bothering you, or bothering you yet, or not bothering you at all--, and GET IT OUT of there.

Yes, I'm saying if your brother is going through, pray for him. Pray what's bothering your brother out of your foundation. If your parents have HBP or some other disease, especially as you watch them age; pray for them, but PRAY IT OUT OF YOUR FOUNDATION. Do it as much for yourself as for your children and your *children's* children. Whether what's in your family's foundation is affecting you or not, if you can see it, do something about it.

You are the third or the fourth generation of somebody in your bloodline. God is coming to visit. He said He would.

So, clean up your foundation and house because GOD is coming to visit. Even if you don't finish the task, be found doing.

With the help of the Holy Spirit clean your own house because God is coming to visit.

So, WHO BEGAT you and who they were spiritually if they left spiritual debt, that is speaking today into your generation. And even further, it is speaking into the 3rd and 4th or more generations of your life and bloodline if you don't do something about it.

It's currently affecting what you do and what happens to you. what you can accomplish and what you can't accomplish. What your life will be like and look like. It is speaking against or for your education. Against or for your career. Against or for your marriage. Against or for your spouse and your kids.

Until what is already programmed by whatever is in your foundation is sorted out, you will get the results that your parents got, that your grandparents got, that your ancestors got... unless there's JESUS.

Unless you let the LORD in—fully into your life. And you must walk upright before the Lord in prayer and spiritual warfare and the Word and disciplines of the Faith, praise and worship and fasting and in giving to change it. Saints, that means *fully in,* not just a little saved for future times, but for right now, fully in Christ.

23. Lord, let me live as though You are visiting every day, every moment, in the Name of Jesus.

24. Lord, do not be a stranger in my life or home, work, or school, in the Name of Jesus.

25. Lord, You are Welcome, in the Name of Jesus.

Earthquakes & Storms

If the foundations be destroyed what can
the righteous do?
(Psalm 11:3)

What destroys a foundation? An earthquake? A storm? In the natural, yeah. But look at all the earthquakes and volcanoes and other natural disasters that are happening in the Earth right now.

Why are bad things happening on Earth or even to Earth? The foundation of Earth needs some help. The foundations of people need some help; all are waiting for the *sons of God* to appear. All of Creation is waiting for the Sons of God to appear. Folks, that's us.

All of Creation is waiting for the Sons of God to appear. We need to speak into Creation, speak into this Earth to heal it because it is being abused, misused by the kingdom of darkness. By witches and warlocks enchanting into the Earth, into the points and factors of Earth, against the people of God. Saints, these activities distress the Earth. The Earth was made to praise God; do you think it likes being re-programmed for evil?

What destroys a foundation? Earthquakes, storms, volcanoes, tsunamis--, but in the spiritual realm parts of your foundation can be destroyed. Anything that is used in a way that God never intended it to be used pollutes and corrupts that thing. It will destroy that thing that is being abused; it will destroy it down to its foundation.

Your foundation is spiritual, so destructive spiritual things can destroy a foundation. So, if stuff is actively destroying your foundation you have to be proactive and counter what is happening. A curse or any evil that is emanating or expressing itself right now is like an active shooter--, and you're doing nothing about it? Any evil in your foundation is an active shooter in your foundation, you have to do something about it – the fact that you have the curse is visited by God and if you are doing nothing about it – too ignorant, too lazy, too scared, want someone else to do it—**then you suffer WHILE you are waiting on the visitation.**

I repeat: You will suffer while you are waiting for the visitation because **your suffering is the notification that you need to be doing something about your life, about your situation, about your condition, about your foundation.** Because God is coming to visit. God will by His Spirit, help you get your life and your place ready for His visit.

When the visitation happens, there is also judgment. Judgment because the stuff was in there and nothing was done about it. God will think you hate Him, and you like the stuff that your ancestors put in there and you want to keep it there.

You don't, *do you?*

If wanting to meet the right person is the thing that is making you look at your foundation, which is a far more serious thing, then so be it. That is a light thing compared to your whole foundation. And how your foundation is affecting others, and your bloodline and the world, and even the Earth--, the entire plan of God.

God may be asking any of us, *Why didn't you do anything about it, because that is what you are put here to do? Be fruitful and multiply, take dominion, and destroy the works of the devil.* The same thing Jesus came here to do and the very same thing He has empowered and instructed us to do, repeating what God has already told us—teaching.

Take dominion over what? Where do you start? At home. Start in your own foundation.

God could be asking any of us, me included, *Why didn't you do what I told you to do?*

He may be asking you, something like, *Didn't you know I didn't want you ignorant?* Didn't He say study to show yourself approved so you can know what's going on? Rightly dividing the Word? Rightly dividing a lie from truth.

God wants to know that you know that Faith without works is dead. Therefore, after you study, take some action.

By Word of Prophecy: God is wanting to know, **Why aren't you doing something to regain *Dominion*?** And then once you have dominion, **Why aren't you doing something <u>IN</u> dominion – doing what you are** supposed to be doing now that you have regained dominion?

God may further want to know: *Why aren't you* occupying *until I come, until I return?*

I didn't mean for this book to be a rebuke, but I am following what the Spirit is leading me to write.

Why aren't you occupying? Why aren't you dealing with your own foundation? Why are you letting your foundation be occupied by strangers, evil *spirits*, interlopers, squatters, and things that are not supposed to be in your foundation? Do you see the *Post-Its*, the evil handwriting of ordinances against what I have said should be in your foundation?

Are you going to let those demons CONTRADICT Me, says the Lord? And you'll do nothing about it?

We are in covenant, when someone rises up against you then I will

fight for you, why aren't you fighting for Me?

Why aren't you doing what I've instructed you to do? is what I hear the Lord asking.

If someone presented a video game to you on your cell phone, computer or game console—wherever you play games, and, that puzzle needed to be solved, you'd surely solve it, wouldn't you? Candy Crush, Royal Flush -- save the king from whatever destruction he's up against today.

The devil is trying to crush all the good things out of your life. He is trying to crush your foundation and take out your bloodline. **You** need to solve it. Solve it out of your bloodline and out of your foundation.

Save the *king*? Baby, you're the *king*. You are the *little k* king in this Earth; save yourself by saving your foundation in prayer and spiritual warfare and walking uprightly in the disciplines of the faith. While being ALL in Christ.

The devil is trying to crush all the good out of your life and bloodline. You have to find out that he is in there causing havoc, how he got there, and then get him out. That is, SOLVE your foundation in prayer and spiritual warfare.

Don't play; slay.

Don't play; slay. Kill all the evil that is in your foundation so it will be easier for you to do the things you need to do in life.

Forget the puzzles for a minute and solve your FOUNDATION. Your life needs to be *solved*: Solve it. That's what God expects.

Lady saints of God: Why have only five of the ten virgins trimmed their lamps? Why are only ½ the people doing what they are supposed to be doing? Or have done what they were supposed to have done to get ready for the bridegroom?

Saints of God why are you not *occupying*? Why are you not using what God has given you to occupy? Take authority and dominion.

The leaders in the house of God, provided they are proper leaders are supposed to be going out into the world with their disciplined congregants to save those that are lost. But we are still saving the people who are at church. When we solve our foundations and arise as sons of God, we will see ourselves equipped to go out and win souls.

You want to meet the right one? Then get yourself ready. Not world ready, but Godly and spiritually ready. Not world-ready, at the gym and the spa and the hair and nail salon, but GODLY and spiritually ready.

26. Lord, give me power and knowledge to solve the problems of my foundation, in the Name of Jesus.

27. Lord, give me Wisdom to rule in Dominion over all the works of Your hands, in the Name of Jesus.

28. Lord, help me to get ready and stay ready, in the Name of Jesus

29. Lord, help me by Your Spirit to be faithful and be found *doing*, in the Name of Jesus.

30. Lord, help me, by Your Spirit to *occupy* until You return, in the Name of Jesus.

WHAT Did They Do?

We don't know what our ancestors have done. Over the millennia, what have your ancestors put into your foundation?

- By their actions?
- By their words?
- By their vows, oaths, affiliations, and alliances.
- By their agreements?
- Did they step into witchcraft or occultism? Then all that is in your foundation. (Most of us don't know.)

If you are not saved and not in Christ most likely they did the same stuff that you have done or are likely to do. The same blueprint is in there if you've not done any foundational work. So, don't be so quick to judge them, if it is a like father like son thing, or a like mother like daughter, it is definitely generational. Saints of God, do not dismiss things that are not of God simply because grandma or daddy was this way. God will not compare you to other humans, when He visits and or judges it will be compared to the Word of God.

Even if you're saved, if you haven't mapped out and cleansed and healed your foundation, and I mean with prayers and spiritual warfare, not with a spiritualist or witchdoctor or New Age person, then you are still subject to your foundation.

I say this: if you had parents that you saw worship and serve the LORD, they read their Bibles daily, prayed separately and together, loved each other, stayed together, taught you and your siblings the Word and the ways of God. They exemplified and walked in it. They

Prayed with you and over you, laid hands on you and blessed you daily, spoke blessings over you and your life daily. If they did all that, and granted, it's a lot, then you should consider that they did all they should have done to minister to you and bring you up in the Lord.

But if they didn't, maybe they didn't do all they were supposed to do to speak into your life and foundation. That could mean that whatever foundation *they* inherited was not changed. If that foundation wasn't evil, then hey—no biggie. But if there was evil in your family's foundation and nothing was addressed, then --, *biggie*.

Maybe you had one parent who did that, well praise the LORD.

If you had one that did and one that didn't, do you realize they canceled each other out? One is doing positive and the other negative. 1000 fighting 1000 equals zero.

Nope don't get mad at anyone, maybe they didn't know to do these things. Are you doing them for your children?

If you are not speaking into **your** children's foundation? Are you speaking into their future, and blessing them and praying for their marriages and their fruitfulness and multiplication and dominion? If not, then what are you doing?

When you've cleansed and mastered your foundation, that's when you've mastered your children's. If not, then it all remains the same or worse, if the devil gets in it. THEY WILL MORE THAN LIKELY, EXCEPT FOR SOME MIRACLE OF GOD HAVE THE SAME RESULTS or worse, if the devil gets in it. They will have the same results that you HAVE OUTSIDE of Jesus CHRIST.

Heal your foundation for your children.

Hear, O heavens, and give ear, O earth: for the Lord hath spoken, I have nourished and brought up children, and they have rebelled against me. (Isaiah 1:2)

The key is to get inside Christ – be saved and get all the way in.

Bless your children. The enemies of God will gladly issue curses to anyone, even your children, so don't you curse your children, yourself. Even if they are getting on your last nerve, there are things you do not EVER say to your children about your children, or *over* your children. EVER.

31. Lord, let me dwell in You and You in me, in the Name of Jesus.

32. Let me be *all in* Christ, in the Name of Jesus.

33. Lord, purge my foundation of every pollution and corruption, in the Name of Jesus.

34.   Lord, heal my foundation, everywhere it needs healing, in the Name of Jesus.

35.   Lord, give me mastery over my foundation, for my sake and for the sake of my generations, in the Name of Jesus.

36.   Lord, bless me to be a blessing to all that I meet and am supposed to bless, and especially to my own children, in the Name of Jesus.

Predestination

Saints of God with or without JESUS you are predestined. With Jesus, you are predestined for good things, salvation, abundance, wholeness and health.

For I know the thoughts that I think toward you, saith the Lord, thoughts of peace, and not of evil, to give you an expected end. (Jeremiah 29:11)

Without Jesus you are predestined to live out what your **blood** says for you to do. If you do not have Christ and are not in Christ what is programmed into your blood is disastrous.

EVEN IF YOU HATE THE STUFF YOUR PARENTS DO OR DID,

OUTSIDE OF CHRIST YOU WILL DO
THE SAME THINGS, EVENTUALLY.

You are predestined to do what
your foundation says for you to do,
outside of Christ. BUT with GOD, being
in Christ and *fully in* you can live the
Abundant life Christ came here for us to
have. Else, you will have to live the life
pre-programmed for you by your
ancestors, whether they knew they were
doing it or not.

37. Lord, have Mercy on me a
sinner. Forgive my sins and the
sins of my parents and my
ancestors, in the Name of Jesus.

The Abortion of Good Things

The early termination of things in your life is caused by a *spirit*. It is not necessarily a one-time action; it is a *spirit*. If you have ever let that *spirit* into your life, it may still be there as a destroyer and a scatterer, ruining projects and good opportunities, as well as relationships and prosperity in your life.

This *spirit* may be instrumental in the ending of relationships too soon. Perhaps God has sent you the right person, but you had a temper tantrum or went into a panic and got out of the relationship prematurely. Jumping to conclusions – all of this hyperactivity could be written in your foundation--, it could be why you act this way. Perhaps you are oversensitive. Perhaps you are prideful and overprotective, don't want to be hurt so you leave people before they can leave you. Does God behave this way? Then what *spirit* is in your soul or in your foundation to make you behave this way? Why are you giving in to it? Could it be because you don't even know it is in you, or influencing you?

Make sure there are no lingering word curses by those who have had or currently have authority to speak over or into your life who pray soulish or diabolical prayers to terminate good things in your life for selfish reasons. Some of those reasons may include because they "love" you so much and don't want you to leave them. Some of those evil prayers may be because you left them, and they don't want you to be with anyone else.

Stay prayed up.

38. *Spirit of abortion* in my life, I terminate you now by the power in the Blood of Jesus. By the Lord and the power of His Christ I command you to uproot yourself and leave my life and my foundation now: I command it, in the Name of Jesus.

39. *Spirits of impatience, agitation, anxiety,* and I want everything now, be gone from my life and foundation, now, in the Name of Jesus.

40. *Spirit of the abortion of good things* in my life, break off of my life and out of my foundation, now, in the Name of Jesus.

41. *Herodian spirit* to terminate good things that have just been born into my life, you DIE, in the Name of Jesus.

42. *Spirit of start but don't finish,* die, in the Name of Jesus.

43. *Spirit of early termination of good things in my life*, die, in the Name of Jesus.

44. Lord Jesus, by Your power restore to me everything that has been lost to me by the foul *spirits of abortion* and the *spirit of abortion of good things* in my life, in the Name of Jesus.

45. Curse of this family can't have nice things, DIE! Die out of my soul and out of my foundation, in the Name of Jesus.

46. Curse of this family, that I cannot have a happy, successful marriage, break and die out of my life and foundation, in the Name of Jesus.

47. Every relationship that has been aborted prematurely, return to me, in the Name of Jesus.

48. Every divine connection that has been aborted either prematurely or before it even happened, return to me, in the Name of Jesus.

49. All fruit of my womb that has been aborted and stolen by this *spirit* or these evil *spirits*, Lord, restore me, Lord recompense me, in the Name of Jesus.

50. All fruit of my labor, all fruit of my hands that has been aborted by this evil *spirit* or any other *spirits* associated with it, Lord return to me all that has been lost, stolen, or destroyed, quickly and suddenly, in the Name of Jesus.

51. Lord, from the devastation by this evil *spirit*, I command a seven-fold restoration, in the Name of Jesus.

Automatic Sacrifices

By the same token, things may be taken from you automatically. If you are complaining that every time you meet someone nice, or every time you get into a promising relationship there is a problem. There may be an ordinance in your foundation that allows that without your even knowing it.

An automatic draft from your bank can be very convenient. Automatic withdrawal from your credit card for a subscription that you don't even use anymore, and you forgot that you even authorized such a thing is not wise stewardship. In this, what we thought would be a good thing turns out to be a problem or wastefulness.

When a certain good thing happens for you or is about to happen, you reach a threshold that the enemy and the curse(s) in your foundation says that you should not pass, so it is automatically taken from you.

Breakthroughs.   Wealth. Relationships. Children--, no, not another cognitive test, but a list of good things that you should have in your life.

Again, we don't know what parents, ancestors, even evil aunts and uncles may have done or authorized. They may have proclaimed your name at an evil altar at any time in your life. Because they are of the same bloodline, they had some authority to do such.

Break every evil dedication over your life, especially those concerning relationships, family, marriage, and children. Reverse every evil exchange that may have been done by a polygamous and/or jealous relative who saw your bright star and wanted it for their dull kid, or for themselves. Elders will steal from the young.

No don't go into the flesh; go into the Spirit and PRAY to reverse any and all of this. If it is not true, your prayer won't hurt a thing. If it is true, not praying will hurt and will keep things as they are, or the situation may worsen.

Déjà Vu?

Lady saints: Why do you keep meeting the same kind of guys?

It's your foundation.

Men: Why do you keep meeting the same kinds of girls?

It's your foundation.

Why can't you find what you really want?

Your foundation.

In your foundation is the blueprint for your life. It is in your BLOOD already it is preprogrammed that you should walk in those ways.

Why do you keep going through the same old stuff? FOUNDATION. Déjà vu? Yes, you not only keep getting the same answer to all these various questions, but you keep meeting the same person. Each time you meet someone new, things seem hopeful, but then they just become who they are, and you begin to see clearly it is the same person all over again.

But you must be prayerful that you are not just getting the same results or poor results while you may have met the right one. Make sure it is not <u>you</u> giving up too early or manifesting a temper tantrum and pushing your divine connection away.

Déjà vu? Ladies especially, if you realize after dating someone for a short time that you are dating someone just like your dad, and that may not be a good thing, that is totally your foundation. If he suddenly starts acting just like your brother, exhibiting traits like your brother that you just can't stand, that's foundation all the way, directing who you can get with, date, or marry. These people act like or even start to look like your relatives? *Ewww!* Gross.

Worse than all that, what will run off a promising suitor is a *spirit spouse.* Do as much warfare as you need to, fast and pray, seek deliverance if necessary and get rid of *spirit spouse.* Yes, this could be a foundational issue: *spirit spouse* could be in your **foundation**. Most *spirit spouses* are of ancestral origin, however individual sin *allows* them. They will be okay with you meeting someone you'll never be serious about, but the moment things start to look like marriage, *spirit spouse* will try to run that suitor away and wreck your relationship.

Heal your foundation so that will change. If not when you finally do realize that this person acts like your relative and they have traits you absolutely cannot stand, one day you may just want to walk away from the marriage. This is not what God intends. God hates broken covenant. So, fix yourself so you can draw what you know you want as a spouse instead of what you've always been around, seen, and what you've always gotten.

(There are a number of prayers against *spirit spouse* on Warfare Prayer Channel on You Tube. Also, the books: **Fantasy Spirit Spouse,** and **Blindsided:** *Has the Old Man Bewitched You?*, among other books by this author. Links at the back of this book)

Frogs & Princes

Ladies: Why do you keep meeting these frogs disguised as princes, or toads who *believe* that they are princes? Who are these guys, anyway?

They are guys with faulty foundations, as well, hopping into your DM's and your life.

We all would do better to stop looking to see how cute somebody is or what their bank account is like and look at the spiritual issues. It's not just about whether you can GET together with that person, or not, but will you **stay** together as a couple? And will you be successful in spiritual things as a couple? Just being successful financially is not what God is about. Just being successful physically is definitely not what God is about. But being successful spiritually, all the other good stuff is in the overflow.

When you roll up on a frog be sure not to kiss them too soon; too much can be stolen in that kiss.

Some people *do* want to be a couple, but they want to do the absolute minimum to be that couple and remain a couple. They want to do the flesh stuff, the physical stuff, the pleasurable stuff, the fun stuff – **BUT THERE IS WORK TO DO—,** spiritual work that must be done to be and remain a successful couple. And that stuff must BE DONE IN TANDEM, THAT IS, **TOGETHER**.

Those who want to be a couple with their own spouse are the people who **want** to be married and be a couple. Those are the ones that God will help. Those are the couples that God will show favor to when that man finds his wife.

Those who do everything separately – they are married on paper for whatever motives they had for that. God is not in that.

But if now you're a couple and it was a great love story—, the greatest amazing, epic and you two had to surmount incredible odds, like a romantic movie, but you did get together, stay together and got married—now what?

What now? If you haven't dealt with any spiritual stuff: if/when your spiritual stuff starts fighting him or his spiritual stuff starts fighting you, or both of your spiritual stuff start fighting each other, what are you going to do then? For example, either or both could have a *spirit spouse*. Either or both could have more than one *spirit spouse*. Those demons will fight and the two of you are the pawns. Your marriage could turn into hell. Unless you deal with *spirit spouse* and get rid of them, they will be working to get rid of the natural spouse.

If the foundation is destroyed, what will the righteous do? The righteous will search out and seek out what is destroying or has destroyed that foundation, and they will root it out and rebuild that foundation properly with Jesus Christ as the Chief Cornerstone. This is especially necessary if *spirit spouse*, for example, was ancestral, that is, already in the foundation. By virtue of now being in either person, if not cast out, it will remain in the foundation and be waiting for your children and your *children's* children.

What else are we talking about here? What else might be in a foundation?

There may be anti-marriage curses in your foundation, which could be why you haven't met that right person you're supposed to marry, or had that divine connection. The *spirit spouse* is the demon sent to enforce the anti-marriage curse.

How will you know?

Look at your family. Are there divorces? Are people not married? Are they miserable in marriage? Are they successful in marriage?

How will you know?

Are **you** married? Are you happily married? Is your spouse also happily married, or are you two in two different marriages in the same marriage? There could be anti-marriage curses in your foundation. There could be divorce ordinances written in your foundation.

Why? Because your ancestors did some foul stuff and this is either a part of the covenant that they made, it is what was traded for what some ancestor got. The trade was that you might never get married, or none of the women in your family would get married, or **stay** married. Perhaps it was that none of the men would get married.

Unless the Holy Spirit tells us exactly what happened and what was said, we may never know. Therefore, this marriage situation, or lack of it is now on the list of things you need to pray about.

As bad as that is, don't get too comfortable, marriage issues may not be all the issues that you see in your family of origin. There could be other stuff as well. As said, it depends on what deals your ancestors made and what they traded, knowingly or unknowingly, with the devil or one of his agents to get something they must have really wanted.

Worse than both those things, the lack of marriage or good marriage candidates in your life, and or in your family might not even be what was traded. Nope. It could be how the demon who has been sent to enforce the evil covenant that your ancestor made has decided to punish you. Your ancestor has not kept up— mainly because he or she is dead and surely told no one about this devil deal--, their dirty, occultic secret.

So, the evil covenant has not been honored. Whatever was promised hasn't been done because no one even knows, except the Holy Spirit. Did you pray; did you ask the Holy Spirit?

1. There was an evil covenant in place.
2. What was supposed to be done to keep these idol *gods* happy?
3. Y'all are all saved now, and you don't serve idol *gods* anymore.

So, the worst could be what is happening and that is that the demon sent to enforce the covenant, by punishing you and your family/bloodline for not keeping their end of the evil deal has decided to jack up the marriages in your bloodline. This on a whim, but also with permission of whatever powers are over this demon or these demons.

SOL (So Out of Luck) there is interest and penalties on something that you didn't even know that you owed, and if you knew you don't have the currency that they trade in to pay it, and you don't even know what currency that is—what do they even want?

And the absolute worst for the *idols* is that you are all now saved, and you don't even deal with idol *gods* anymore.

But the best thing for you is now you are saved, and you are in Christ Jesus. You are *all in*. Now, you can deal with these idols and demons and *little g, gods* **in Christ**, in spiritual warfare, in intercession, in corporate and individual prayers.

There may be anti-progress curses in your foundation. How do you know? Are you making progress or not? If you're not making progress, then who will want to marry you if you're broke? It's not the only thing, but it is important that you can take care of your family.

Like secondhand smoke, you are not smoking or vaping, but you are in the smokey haze of the person who is, or did—your ancestors lit up, it seems and left a haze of smoke and iniquity in your foundation.

52. Lord, forgive the sins of my parents and my ancestors, and by Your great Mercy remove all iniquity from my foundation, in the Name of Jesus.

53. Every wanna-be prince who is really a frog, hop out of my life along with the power that sent you, in the Name of Jesus.

54. Every frog who thinks you are a prince, go back and heal your foundation, then holler back later, if the Lord agrees, in the Name of Jesus.

55. Every wanna-be princess who is really a frog, hop out of my life, along with the power that sent you, in the Name of Jesus.

56. Every frog who thinks you are a princess, go back, heal your foundation then holler back later, if the Lord agrees, in the Name of Jesus.

57. Every power that sent a frog to me as a curse, take your frog back, return to sender, and let your powers die, in the Name of Jesus.

58. Lord, make me one of Your 7000, curseless, frog-less, but instead, blessed, married, and multiplying, in the Name of Jesus.

Similarly, not meeting the right person to be married to, not getting married may not even be the curse or the issue, it is anti-progress curses in your bloodline. Can you even believe how twisted and contorted this all is? So, to break free of all this, pray the obvious, but sometimes you have to pray for more than the obvious to be set free of foundational curses and bondages.

Continue praying, but now hit the anti-progress curses. Generally, pray against all curses to cover whatever is ailing you as to why you haven't met and married your beloved yet. Or, why you are married but suffering instead of enjoying your *boo*.

>59. Every anti-progress and anti-prosperity curse over my life and in my foundation, break and die, in the Name of Jesus.

There may be anti-education curses in your foundation.

How do you know?

Did you get the right education? Did you get the education that you wanted? Is your education being used to the full so you can live a pleasant stress-free life? All of that will affect your ability to get married, stay married and be successful in marriage, and bring forth righteous seed. It is a cascade of events.

60. Every anti-education curse in my foundation or family line, break, in the Name of Jesus.

61. Any power who has captured my degrees and certificates, loose them, loose them, loose them now, so that I may prosper, in the Name of Jesus.

Who Begat You?

Why do some people, even some races seem to get ahead more, or more easily than others? It's FOUNDATION.

Where do you come from? You need to know. What is the foundation of YOUR PEOPLE? You need to know. Who *begat* you?   What were they about, spiritually? **You need to know.**

There are those who seem to have easier lives, their foundation is different, it just *is*. They may have an easier or more difficult time than you, just making it in life. It's not like they are doing anything against you, if they are not spiritual, they won't understand that life is harder for you, or why it is more difficult.

Still, to you the world is unfair.

If you have a right foundation, and you walk upright before the Lord, then everything will work to your favor. After you have cleansed and purged your foundation and it is now pristine, spiritually speaking then you will walk in the promises of God. The Grace of God. The Divine Favor of the Lord.

Then, will you say it is unfair? No, you won't because it will be to your favor. Favor is not fair.

62. Lord, by your Grace and Mercy, forgive the sins, sin debt, and iniquity of all who begat me, in the Name of Jesus.

63. Lord, by the power in the Blood of Jesus blot out and remove all pollution, corruption, and iniquity from my foundation so that I may prosper, in the Name of Jesus.

What To Do

    A. Get saved.

    B. Get filled with the Holy Spirit.

    C. REPENT for yourself and your entire bloodline.

You don't know what they've done or what they've inadvertently put into your family's foundation. And now you're suffering because tag, you're it--, you are the next generation to have to live through the curses in your foundation. You don't know what is stuck in there or growing in there, unless the Holy Spirit shows you.

    D. Presume that everything that is in there needs to be healed and prayed about.

Pray for a healed foundation, getting rid of all the destructive stuff that is blocking you from having an abundant life, getting the career you enjoy that prospers you and the plan of God for your life.

Get married to the right person the first time. And even if it's not the first time, getting married this time and staying married. Having righteous seed. At least putting yourself in position to have righteous seed.

Sow into the lives of your children--, not buying them everything they want, but sowing spiritually into them. Speak over them and prophesy over your children. Lay hands on them, anoint them. Pray with them and over them and for them, in the Name of Jesus. Pray for others, as well to have a prosperous and abundant life. Most definitely, bring forth and minister to your righteous seed.

Look on You Tube for Warfare Prayer Channel to *Heal Your Foundation.* There are prayers on both my channels for marriage.

Why are you meeting the same fellows over and over? Because in your foundation, in your blood, in your DNA that is what has been assigned to you.

If you have the eyesight and the vision and the Wisdom to say, *I don't like that--,* then that is a start. If you don't like and reject the types that you're meeting, then that is discernment.

When you repeatedly don't like who is approaching you. Do you feel like you have been blocked from the real people you are supposed to meet? **Then do your foundation work.**

What you don't like and can't accept is what is sent in to block you from who you are really supposed to meet. The Blockers. That is what is in your blood and your foundation, so that is what you draw, absent Christ.

These frogs? That's what's in your foundation. Oh, *these* frogs.

Worse, maybe YOU are *these frogs–,* and you are what is in **their** foundation, and that's why they are coming to find you. Maybe that's why they are seeking you. You are what is in their foundation—so they find you, because they think you are their level.

The old guys, the married ones, the ones that aren't about anything but the flesh. The ones that want to take from you. The ones that want to get things from you.

If you are in *their* foundation, they will be looking for **you**. If you don't like them, then change your foundation; heal it.

You don't know what's in their foundation. How do you not know that in some people's foundations that they can only marry a witch or a warlock? If they are looking for you, make sure you're not that.

How do you know that there are not curses in your foundation that you should only be attracted to a witch or warlock? You'd better make sure. You'd better pray.

There could be curses so foul that you can't even guess what the evil incantation was that put that curse in your foundation. And, it wouldn't have landed unless there was a cause—unless there was iniquity and sin.

So, PRAY AGAINST everything. And be sure to repent and always ask for Mercy.

(More on this in the book, **Level the Playing Field** by this author.)

Be Sure to Repent

Change you so you will change what you attract.

Change you and you will attract different fellows, ladies.

CHANGE you and attract different ladies, fellows.

Be serious and GOD will get in it. God runs the marriage service for those who are in the Kingdom of Heaven and want to marry, be fruitful, multiply and serve the KINGDOM of Heaven.

The devil runs the dating service for those who want to service their flesh. So, who are you praying to? Keep it real. If you want to get into a relationship and stay in it, then be serious about this.

However, you need to be real, be you to keep the relationship.

You need to be discerning spiritually to keep your relationship. You don't think that just because you two got together and got married that the attacks are going to stop, do you? They don't stop, they won't just stop because you MET.
Oh no. But now you have a bazooka and not just a BB gun

Not that putting 1000 angels to flight was small—that was huge on its own. But —with the two of you together you have a bazooka. So be prepared, be unified and fire back at the devil. Don't be sitting ducks. Don't be victims.

Until you are in Christ and **fully in**, you will not be able to resist your own foundation--, you can't. What has been programmed into it by your ancestors— by their words, by their actions, by their iniquity and their sin debt. You never met these people, but this is what they left for you.

So, do you like your cuteness or your little figure, your pretty skin and healthy hair? That's surface stuff. You think you're the man; you like your biceps and your height and think you're handsome?

That's nice. That's surface stuff. But if you want to rejoice in those things that you inherited by DNA from your folks, then rejoice, be happy.

Or maybe you don't like what you look like--, what you've inherited by DNA and you've been changing it ever since you knew you could with makeup and diet and exercise and whatever you could use to change that to suit you. As long as it is in line with what God said you can do-- how you look--, you've changed that; but all that is surface.

Why haven't you changed your foundation?

MORE IMPORTANTLY, you need to look deep, deep, deep to see what else you inherited, spiritually and deal with it.

LET'S PRAY

64. Father, hear my repentance today; I repent for all my sins, the sins of my parents and my ancestors—all those who *begat* me, all the way back to Adam and Eve, please have MERCY. Remove all iniquity from our bloodline, in the Name of Jesus.

65. Lord, have Mercy on me, a sinner. Accept me in the Beloved so that I may live and prosper all to the praise of Your Glory, in the Name of Jesus.

66. Lord, make me serious about marriage and fruitfulness, multiplying and having dominion in the Earth, in the Name of Jesus.

67. Lord, heal my foundation, cast out everything that is in it that has not been put there by You and all that is not like You or *of* You, cast it out, in the Name of Jesus.

68. I RENOUNCE ANY MARRIAGE OR AGREEMENT BETWEEN MY DESTINY AND THE ANCESTRAL ALTARS OF MY FATHER'S HOUSE, IN THE NAME OF JESUS.

69. I RENOUNCE ANY MARRIAGE OR AGREEMENT BETWEEN MY DESTINY AND THE ANCESTRAL ALTARS OF MY MOTHER'S HOUSE, IN THE NAME OF JESUS.

70. EVERY MARK OF EVIL OCCURRENCE IN MY BUSINESS, MINISTRY, and LIFE BE REMOVED BY THE BLOOD OF JESUS CHRIST.

71. EVERY MARK OF LATE MARRIAGE IN MY LIFE, BE DESTROYED BY THE FIRE OF GOD, IN THE NAME OF JESUS.

72. Every *spirit spouse* in my life or foundation be burned beyond recognition and further function by the FIRE, Fire, FIRE of the Holy Ghost, and die, in the Name of Jesus.

73. I RELEASE THE FIRE OF THE HOLY GHOST against all the spiritual mirrors, tapes, cameras, satellites, and every evil device that the devil has set to monitor my life, marriage, and ministry.

74. IN THE NAME OF JESUS, i cancel and nullify all the spells, curses, evil prayers, enchantments, and psychic commands that have been made against my foundation, my life, my marriage and ministry.

75. IN THE NAME OF JESUS CHRIST OF NAZARETH, I BREAK THE SEASONS OF POVERTY, HUNGER, AND DROUGHTS OVER MY LIFE.

76. I am blessed. I am fruitful. I am in multiplication regarding the Godly things in my life, in the Name of Jesus.

77. I take dominion over the fish of the sea, the fowls of the air and over every living thing in this Earth, in the Name of Jesus.

78. I arise as a son of God, Amen.

79. I am in Christ. I am in CHRIST. I am in CHRIST. I am fully in, in the Name of Jesus.

80. I receive and keep all Divine Connections that pertain to my relationships, dating, and marriage life, in the Name of Jesus.

81. I seal these declarations across every realm, dimension age, timeline past present and future to infinity. I seal them with the Blood of Jesus and the Holy Spirit of Promise.

82. Any backlash planned or attempted against this word or prayers for any readers or prayers, backfire against the sender 1000 times and to infinity, in the Name of Jesus.

AMEN

Dear Reader

Thank you for acquiring and reading this book. You will surely meet the right ones after changing yourself by changing your foundation. Do not delay. What God planned for you and promised you can be yours.

In the Name of Jesus, **Amen.**

Dr. Marlene Miles

Related titles (new) **Love Breaks Your Heart** https://a.co/d/1F9l5AB

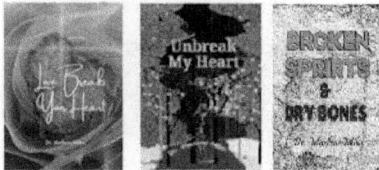

Unbreak My Heart: Don't Let Me Die

https://a.co/d/bH9XAFE

Broken Spirits & Dry Bones
https://a.co/d/52kZgEX

Prayer books by author

While most books by this author have prayer points either throughout the book or at the end, there are some books that are **only** prayers. You just open up the book and pray. They are listed below:

Prayers Against Barrenness: *For Success in Business and Life*

Fruit of the Womb: *Prayers Against Barrenness*

Beauty Curses, *Warfare Prayers Against*
https://a.co/d/5Xlc2OM

Courts of Marriage: Prayers for Marriage in the Courts of Heaven
(prayerbook) https://a.co/d/cNAdgAq

Courtroom Warfare @ Midnight
(prayerbook) https://a.co/d/5fc7Qdp

Demonic Cobwebs *(prayerbook)*
https://a.co/d/fp9Oa2H

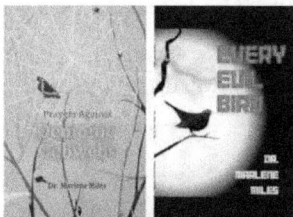

Every Evil Bird https://a.co/d/hF1kh1O

Every Evil Arrow
https://a.co/d/afgRkiA

Gates of Thanksgiving

Call Down Fire (new!)
https://a.co/d/hN7kGnE

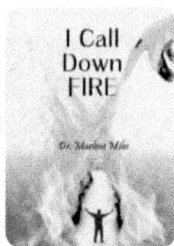

Spirits of Death & the Grave, Pass Over Me and My House
https://a.co/d/dS4ewyr

Please note that my name is spelled incorrectly on amazon, but not on the book.

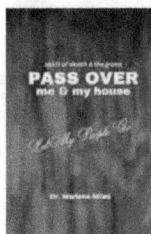

Throne of Grace: Courtroom Prayer

https://a.co/d/fNMxcM9

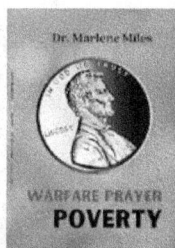

Warfare Prayer Against Poverty
https://a.co/d/bZ61lYu

Other books by this author

AK: *The Adventures of the Agape Kid*

AMONG SOME THIEVES

Ancestral Powers https://a.co/d/9prTyFf

Backstabbers https://a.co/d/gi8iBxf

Barrenness, *Prayers Against*
https://a.co/d/feUltIs

Battlefield of Marriage, *The*

Blindsided: *Has the Old Man Bewitched You?*
https://a.co/d/5O2fLLR

Break Free from Collective Captivity

Casting Down Imaginations
https://a.co/d/1UxlLqa

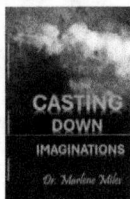

Churchcraft: Witchcraft In the Church

Churchzilla, The Wanna-Be, Supposed-to-be
Bride of Christ

Curses of Blind Men

Demonic Cobwebs (prayerbook)

Demonic Time Bombs

Demons Hate Questions

Devil Loves Trauma, *The*

Devil Weapons: Unforgiveness, Bitterness,...

The Devourers: *Thieves of Darkness 2*

Do Not Swear by the Moon

Don't Refuse Me, Lord (4 book series)

https://a.co/d/idP34LG

Dream Defilement

The Emptiers: *Thieves of Darkness,* 1
https://a.co/d/5I4n5mc

Every Evil Arrow https://a.co/d/afgRkiA

Evil Touch https://a.co/d/gSGGpS1

Failed Assignment https://a.co/d/3CXtjZY

Fantasy Spirit Spouse
https://a.co/d/hW7oYbX

FAT Demons (The): *Breaking Demonic Curses*

The Fold (5-book series)

- The Fold (Book 1)
- Name Your Seed (Book 2)
- The Poor Attitudes of Money (3)
- Do Not Orphan Your Seed (4)
- For the Sake of the Gospel (5)
- My Sowing Journal

Gang Ups: *Touch Not God's Anointed*

got HEALING? Verses for Life

got LOVE? Verses for Life

got HOPE? Verses for Life

got money? https://a.co/d/g2av41N

How to Dental Assist

How to Dental Assist2: Be Productive, Not
Wasteful

I Take It Back

Legacy

Let Me Have A Dollar's Worth
https://a.co/d/h8F8XgE

Level the Playing Field

Living for the NOW of God

Lose My Location https://a.co/d/crD6mV9

Love Breaks Your Heart

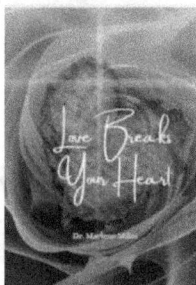

Man Safari, *The*

Marriage Ed. Rules of Engagement &
Marriage

Made Perfect in Love

Money Hunters: Beware of Those

Money on the Altar https://a.co/d/4EqJ2Nr

Mulberry Tree https://a.co/d/9nR9rRb

Motherboard (The) - *Soul Prosperity Series*

Name Your Seed

Occupy: *Until I Return*

Plantation Souls

Players Gonna Play

Power Money: Nine Times the Tithe

https://a.co/d/gRt41gy

The Power of Wealth *(forthcoming)*

Powers Above

Remember the Time https://a.co/d/3PbBjkF

Repent of Visiting Evil Altars
https://a.co/d/3n3Zjwx

The Robe, *Part 1, The Lessons of Joseph*

The Robe, *The Lessons of Joseph* Part II,

Seasons of Grief

Seasons of Waiting

Seasons of War

Second Marriage, Third--, *Any Marriage*

https://a.co/d/6m6GN4N

Seducing Spirits: *Idolatry & Whoredoms*

Sift You Like Wheat

Six Men Short: What Has Happened to all the Men?

Soul Prosperity, Soul Prosperity Series Book 3
https://a.co/d/5p8YvCN

Soulish & Diabolical Prayer Treatment

Souls In Captivity, Soul Prosperity Series Book 2

The Spirit of Poverty

StarStruck

SUNBLOCK

The Swallowers: *Thieves of Darkness*, Book 3

Take It Back

This Is NOT That: How to Keep Demons from Coming at You

Time Is of the Essence

Too Many Wives: *Why You Have Lady Problems*

Tormenting Spirits   https://a.co/d/dAogEJf

Toxic Souls

Triangular Power *(series)*

- Powers Above
- SUNBLOCK
- Do Not Swear by the Moon
- STARSTRUCK

Uncontested Doom

Unguarded Hours, *The*

Unseen Life, *The* https://a.co/d/0drZ5Ll

Upgrade: How to Get Out of Survival Mode

- Toxic Souls (Book 2 of series)
- Legacy (Book 3 of series)

The Wasters: *Thieves of Darkness,* Bk 2
https://a.co/d/bUvI9Jo

What Have You to Declare? What Do You Have With You from Where You've Been?

When I Was A Child, *I Prayed As a Child*

When the Devourer is Rebuked

https://a.co/d/1HVv8oq

The Wilderness Romance *(series)* This
series is about conducting a Godly
relationship and marriage with someone who
is a Wilderness person. It is about how to
recognize it and navigate through it. These
books are about how not to get caught up in
such.

- *The Social Wilderness*
- *The Sexual Wilderness*
- *The Spiritual Wilderness*

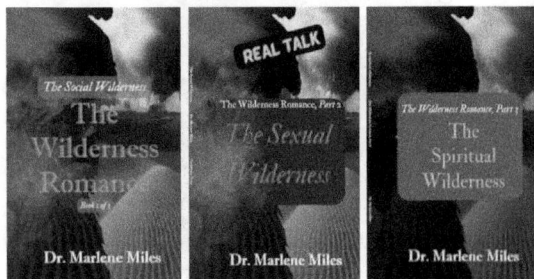

Other Series

The Fold (a series on Godly finances)
https://a.co/d/4hz3unj

Soul Prosperity Series https://a.co/d/bz2M42q

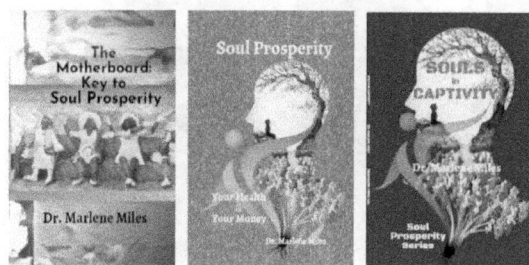

Spirit Spouse books

https://a.co/d/9VehDSo

Thieves of Darkness series

Triangular Powers https://a.co/d/aUCjAWC

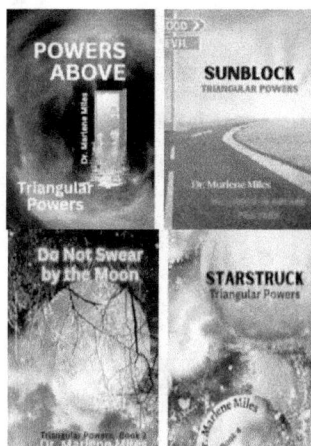

Upgrade (series) *How to Get Out of Survival Mode* https://a.co/d/aTERhXO

Notes